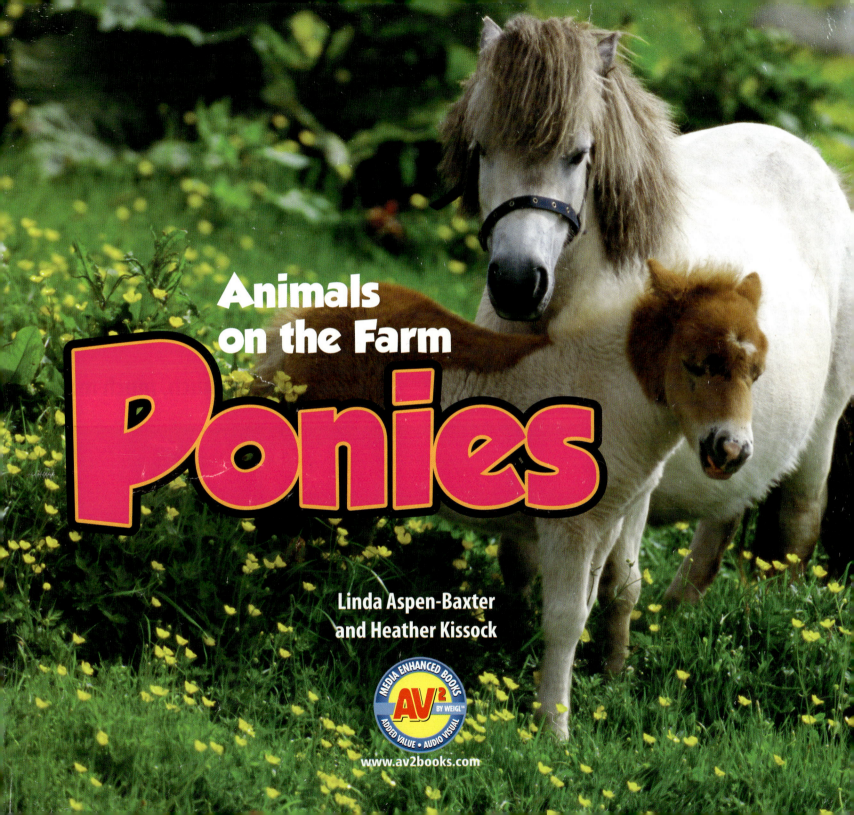

Animals
on the Farm

Ponies

Linda Aspen-Baxter
and Heather Kissock

www.av2books.com

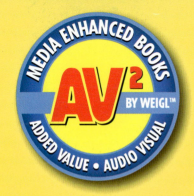

MEDIA ENHANCED BOOKS
AV²
BY WEIGL™
ADDED VALUE • AUDIO VISUAL

Go to **www.av2books.com**, and enter this book's unique code.

BOOK CODE

V568773

AV² by Weigl brings you media enhanced books that support active learning.

AV² provides enriched content that supplements and complements this book. Weigl's AV² books strive to create inspired learning and engage young minds in a total learning experience.

Your AV² Media Enhanced books come alive with...

Audio
Listen to sections of the book read aloud.

Video
Watch informative video clips.

Embedded Weblinks
Gain additional information for research.

Try This!
Complete activities and hands-on experiments.

Key Words
Study vocabulary, and complete a matching word activity.

Quizzes
Test your knowledge.

Slide Show
View images and captions, and prepare a presentation.

... and much, much more!

Published by AV² by Weigl
350 5th Avenue, 59th Floor
New York, NY 10118
Website: www.av2books.com   www.weigl.com

Library of Congress Cataloging-in-Publication Data

Kissock, Heather.
 Ponies / Heather Kissock and Linda Aspen-Baxter.
    p. cm. -- (Animals on the farm)
 ISBN 978-1-61690-929-1 (hardcover : alk. paper) -- ISBN 978-1-61690-575-0 (online)
 1. Ponies--Juvenile literature. I. Aspen-Baxter, Linda. II. Title.
 SF315.K57 2012
 636.1'6--dc23
                          2011023423

Printed in the United States of America in North Mankato, Minnesota
1 2 3 4 5 6 7 8 9 0 15 14 13 12 11

062011
WEP030611

Senior Editor: Heather Kissock   Art Director: Terry Paulhus

Weigl acknowledges Getty Images as the primary image supplier for this title.

Animals on the Farm

Ponies

CONTENTS

3

4

I am a small horse. Farmers keep me to ride and pull things.

5

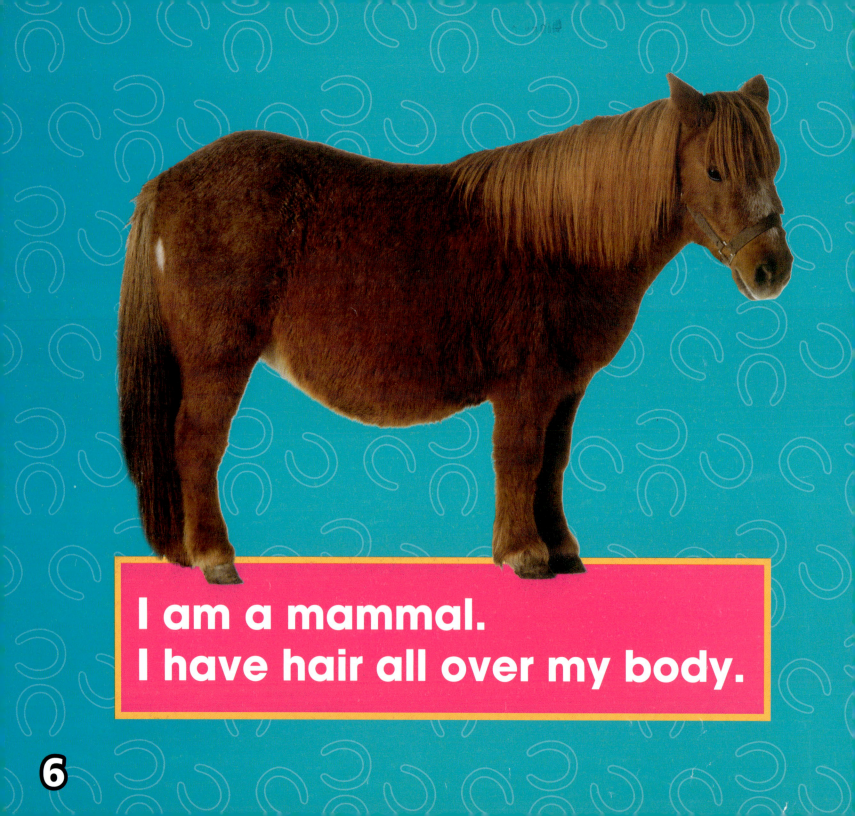

I am a mammal.
I have hair all over my body.

6

I use my four strong legs to walk and run. I have hooves at the end of my legs.

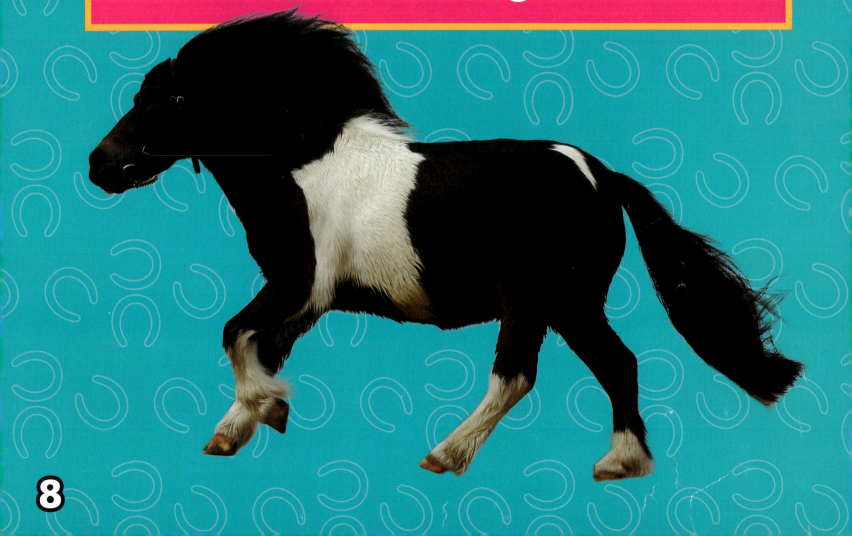

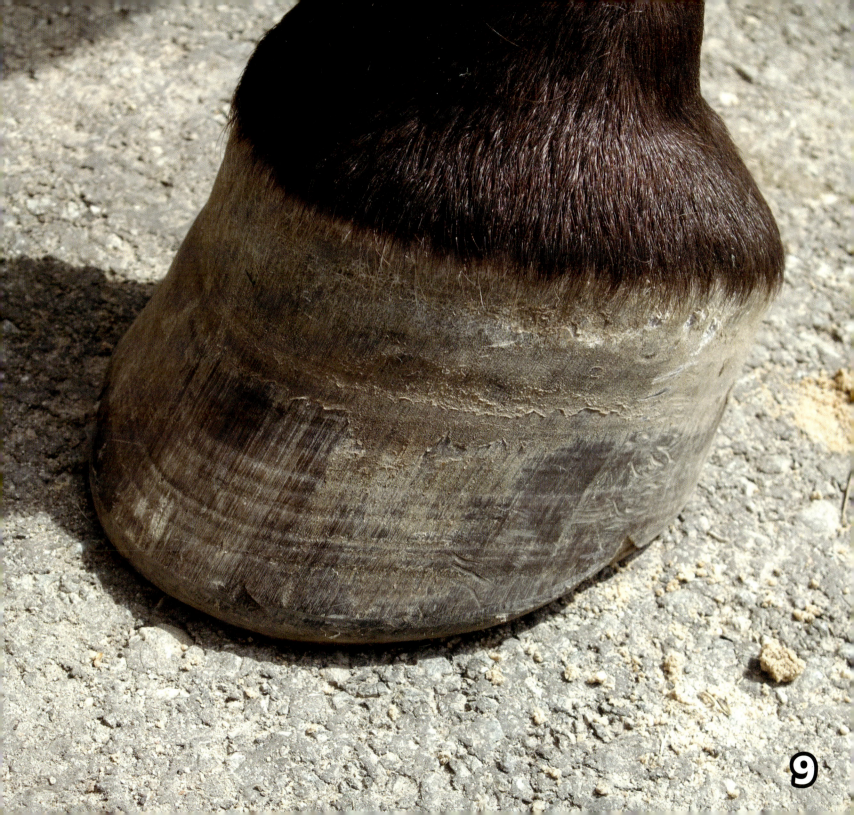

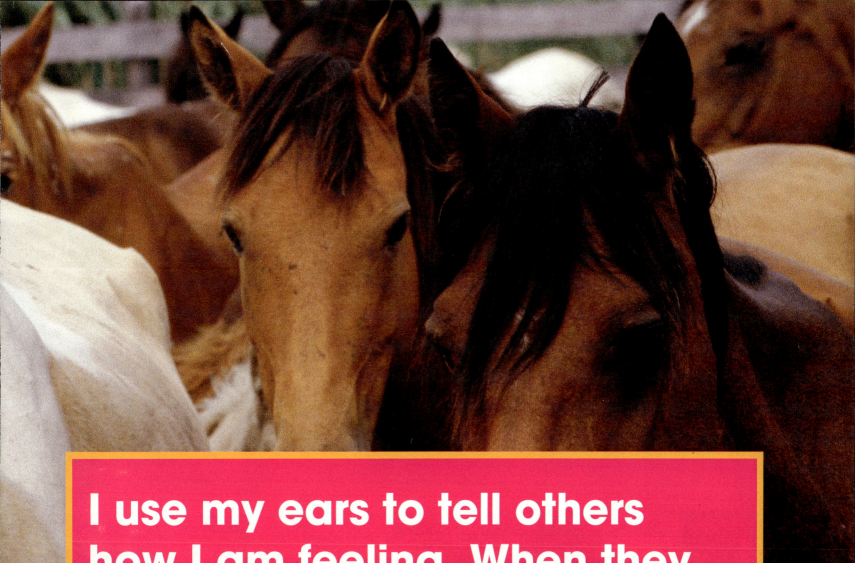

I use my ears to tell others how I am feeling. When they are forward and pointing up, I am happy.

I eat grass, hay, and grains. Carrots are a special treat for me.

12

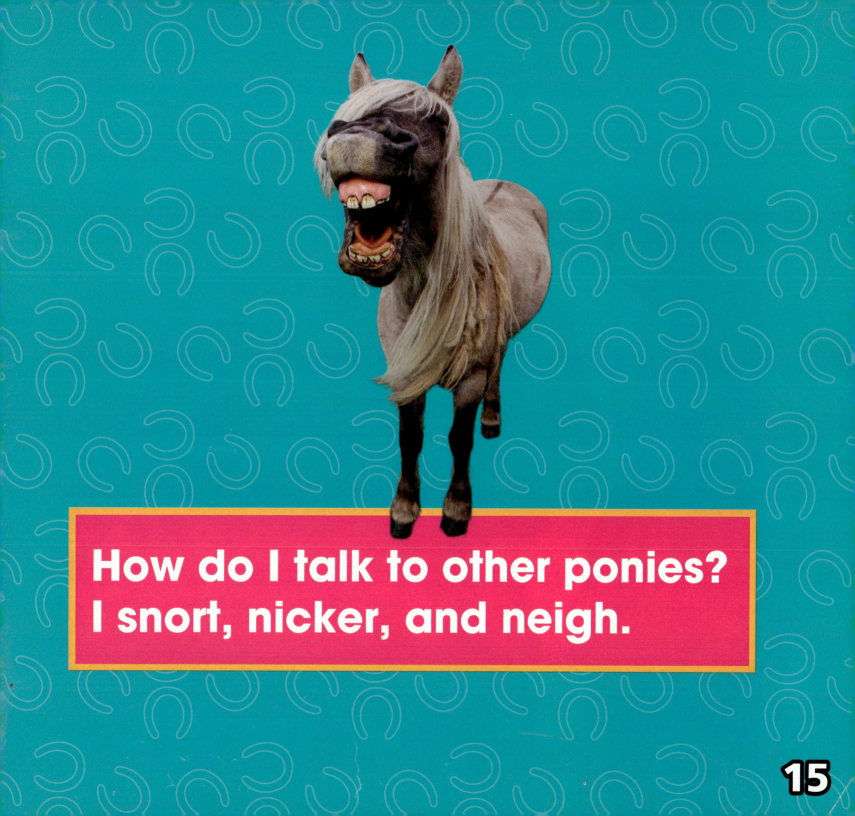

**How do I talk to other ponies?
I snort, nicker, and neigh.**

15

I like to be with other ponies. We run around and play with each other.

17

I sometimes have a baby in the spring.

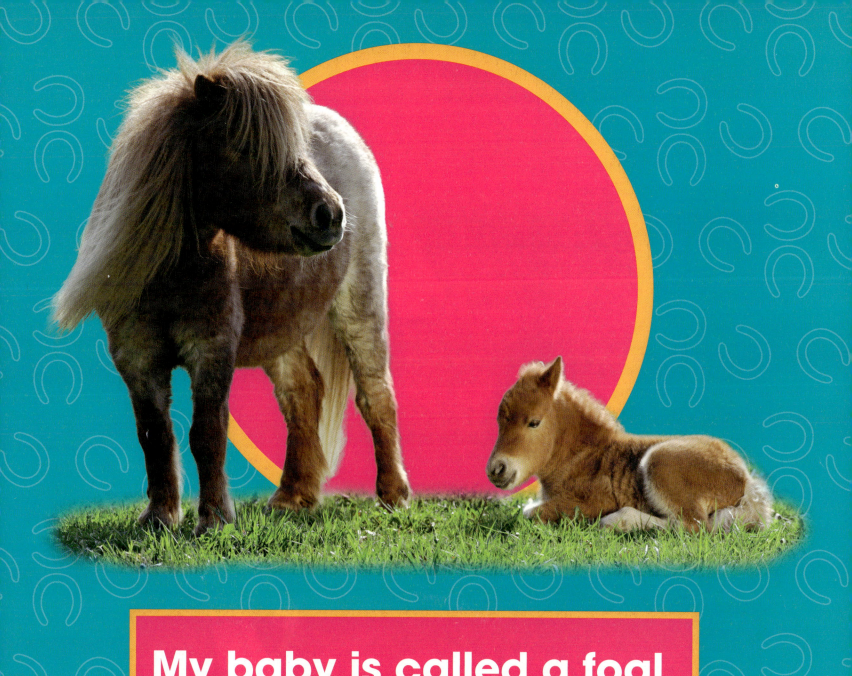

My baby is called a foal.

My baby can walk shortly after it is born. Its legs are very wobbly at first.

21

PONY FACTS

This page provides more detail about the interesting facts found in the book. Simply look at the corresponding page number to match the fact.

Pages 4–5

Farmers keep ponies to ride and pull things. Ponies are small horses. They stand less than 57 inches (1.5 meters) tall. In the past, they pulled carts and carried armies into battle. Today, some people use ponies as pack animals to carry goods. Others ride ponies for fun and for sport. Some people even keep ponies as service animals.

Pages 6–7

Ponies are mammals. Mammals have three main features. One of the most obvious is that they have hair or fur all over their body. Mammals are also warm-blooded. This means that are able to generate their own body heat. Finally, female mammals are able to feed their young with milk from their bodies.

Pages 8–9

Ponies use their legs to walk and run. They have hooves at the end of each leg. Hooves are horn-like shells that protect the soft parts of a pony's feet. Ponies are athletic animals that need to run freely. Their bodies are adapted to living on open plains and pasture lands. A pony's strong, muscular legs need exercising daily.

Pages 10–11

Ponies use their ears to tell others how they are feeling. The position and movement of the ears indicates the pony's mood and its intentions. A happy pony points its ears forward. An angry pony flattens its ears backward. When ponies flick their ears back and forth, they are listening to the sounds around them.

Pages 12–13

Ponies eat grass, hay, and grains. Ponies are herbivores. This means they eat plants. Working ponies need high-energy feed, such as special grains and hay. Carrots and sugar cubes are treats for ponies. Ponies should always have fresh water nearby to drink.

Pages 14–15

Ponies snort, nicker, and neigh to talk to other ponies. Each sound has a special meaning. A nicker is a soft grunt. It is used to say hello to a pony that is nearby. Neighs are loud calls. A pony will neigh to send a warning to other ponies. A pony snorts when it is unsure of a situation.

Pages 16–17

Ponies like to be with other ponies. Ponies are social animals. Many live in large groups called herds. In herds, some ponies are leaders, while others are followers. The leaders are the first to access food, water, and mates.

Pages 18–19

Ponies have their babies in the spring. A female pony carries her babies for about 11 months. She generally gives birth to one foal each year. The process of giving birth is called foaling. Male foals are called colts, and female foals are called fillies.

Pages 20–21

Foals can walk shortly after they are born. At birth, a foal's legs are almost full-grown. Foals can begin to walk about 20 minutes after they are born. Foals grow quickly and are considered to be full-grown by the time they are three years old.

WORD LIST

Research has shown that as much as 65 percent of all written material published in English is made up of 300 words. These 300 words cannot be taught using pictures or learned by sounding them out. They must be recognized by sight. This book contains 47 common sight words to help young readers improve their reading fluency and comprehension. This book also teaches young readers several important content words. These words are paired with pictures to aid in learning and improve understanding.

Page	Sight Words First Appearance
5	a, and, I, keep, me, small, things, to
6	all, have, my, over
8	at, end, four, of, run, the, use, walk
11	are, how, others, they, tell, up, when
12	eat, for
15	do, talk
17	around, be, each, like, play, we, with
18	in, sometimes
19	called, is
21	after, can, first, it, very

Page	Content Words First Appearance
4	farmers, horse
6	body, hair, mammal
8	hooves, legs
11	ears
12	carrots, grains, grass, hay, treat
15	ponies
18	baby, spring
19	foal

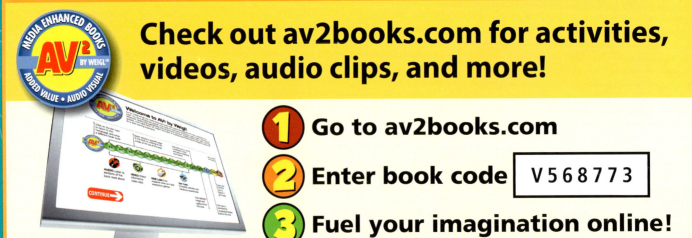